**Sinking
Under
Tension**

Words by
T.W.Benz
Photography by
Dan Harrison

Forever

Scarred by all my thoughts
                    Is this time for order?
Thinking beyond my grasp
                    My time shrinking shorter.

To hell with all the rhymes and all the time

I only need this moment

                    Cause Forever
                    I Shall Find
                    My Oceans Endless

Sinking Under Tension

The beauty of her shoulders
The taste of her lips
The tightness of my chest
Losing her in this maze

Life, Love, Emotions

Spirits of this love
Playing hide and seek

Beauty through my shell
Walking through this hell

Sinking
Under
Tension

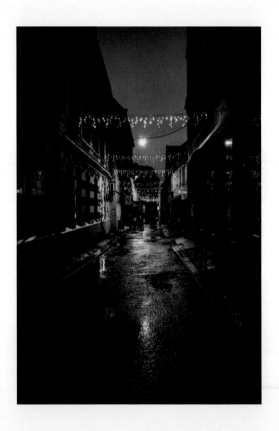

There Are Times
There are moments when the earth beneath you gives way,
And the ground feels colder, heavier than a universe collapsing inward.

Pain, vast and consuming, is a private comedy to the distant watcher.
You're a lone figure in a silent theater,
Hurt without solace, hope without light,
No hands to catch you, no warmth to embrace.

                                        The void
                                presses in;

A quiet interrogation of how and why.
Some wail into the unanswering dark,
Some laugh like madness,
Others crumble, fold into themselves,

While a few
        Oh, a few stand in unshaken stillness.
                In this fracture of time,

Path splinters
To think
How did I fall?
A loop of doubt and futility,

Chasing shadows of blame,
Circling endlessly in the ruins of a moment.

Or to think
How do I rise?
A rebellion born not of strength but emptiness,
The fire of movement sparked by the cold absence of all else.
The hours, the years,
They will pound their drums against you.
Their rhythm does not stop.

But you,
        You can choose:

                    To rise with no reason

                                            but rising
                                    itself.

He Is Gone
The door swung shut, and the light grew thin,
A battle of silence I could never win.
                    The sun still burned, but its warmth had died,
                    As shadows consumed the hope inside.
No words were spoken, no goodbye was said,
Just the echoes of silence that filled my head.
                    The weight of his absence, a cruel refrain,
                    An unyielding tether of invisible pain.
Years have passed, yet I stand here still,
A prisoner bound by a vanished will.
                    I relive that moment, the quake, the sting,
                    The shattering silence his leaving did bring.

            He walked away with no scream, no cry,
            His stillness spoke what words deny.

A quiet so loud, it tore me apart,
A soundless thunder within my heart.

                    What cuts deeper? The void or the quest?
                    The questions unanswered, the ache in my chest?

His silence persists, a melody wrong,
A haunting refrain where he once belonged.

Simple Rule
Life is a knife fight, sharp and bare.
No room for hesitation, no breath to spare.

> Blades clash in the quiet,
> striking with purpose.
> A dance as ancient,
> as the ground
> beneath your feet.

The rule is simple: someone must fall.
Loss is inevitable; the air hums with its certainty.

It is not the sharpness of the blade that matters,
> But the resolve of the one holding it.

There are no referees, no hands to intervene.
The ground absorbs the echoes of struggle.

Unshaped by fairness.
A moment to decide who stays and who bleeds.

> And mercy is a shadow,
> that never arrives.

Worlds Within
The best worlds do not ask for your eyes;
They beckon in the quiet, where sight surrenders to wonder.

Close them,
and the shapes emerge.

A realm of whispers, glowing with the hues of imagination.
These worlds hum with unspeakable textures,
Where rivers of thought carve valleys in the soul,
And mountains rise, built from the sediment of dreams.

The air is softer, a language you can only feel.
No map can guide you here,
No compass dares to measure the distance.

These are not places for the body,
They are sanctuaries for the unseen.

Close your eyes,
The horizon unfolds,
Vast expanse born from the rhythm of your heartbeat.

The best worlds do not wait for you to find them;
They are already within.

Shouting When Angry

Under the glow of a moon draped in silver light,
The master and pupil sat, wrapped in the velvet of night.
The air was still, the earth bathed in a sacred calm,
As if the universe itself had whispered a psalm.
"Tell me, my student," the master began,
"Why do humans shout when anger takes command?
Why, when they're near, does the voice rise high,
As though their words need wings to touch the sky?"
The pupil thought, his brow lined with care,
The weight of the question hanging heavy in the air.
"Perhaps, dear master, when anger takes hold,
The calmness between hearts grows distant and cold."
The master smiled, his gaze soft as a stream,
His voice a melody, like a fading dream.
"True, but the answer goes deeper still,
Let me paint the picture, if you will.

When hearts are bound, close in their song,
The space between them feels tender, not wrong.
But when anger flares, it drives hearts apart,
A rift is born, tearing soul from heart.
In this distance, their voices must leap,
Over a chasm so vast, over wounds that seep.
The louder they shout, the more they try,
To bridge what's broken, though they don't know why.
But when love reigns, there's no need for sound,
No words required where peace is found.
Eyes can whisper what lips cannot say,
And silence itself becomes their way.
For two hearts aligned, no storm can sever,
Their bond speaks softly, forever and ever.
So, remember this truth, let it light your way,
Shouting builds distance; love lets you stay."

Dear Darling

Dear darling,
The world bends in curves you seem to command,
A shadowless sun, a wave carving sand.
I chase your echo through uncharted skies,
A tether to dreams where eternity lies.
Dear darling,
Words dissolve before they can form,
A vaporous hymn in a thunderstorm.
You're the pulse in the void, the silence between,
The colour unseen in the spectrum's sheen.
Dear darling,
Your name is a star that no map can define,
A flicker that dances beyond time's line.
I draw your outline in the absence of light,
A whisper of dawn in the deep of night.
Dear darling,
You fracture the clock, make stillness bloom,
Each moment a spiral, a folding room.
I speak your name, but it tears at my breath,
A paradox living at the edge of death.

Stay, dear darling, and rewrite my air. A mosaic of chaos I long to wear.
You are not the muse nor the ink in my veins. But the cipher of life that my
chaos contains.

Time

Tick.
The clock whispers its rhythm,
But in truth, time does not move.
It waits.
Stretching each moment into an eternity,
A blade hovering just above the skin.
Tock.
A sound that fractures the air,
Each interval a chasm, each silence a scream.
Time becomes elastic,
Pulling memories through its unyielding grip.

Tick.
The blade presses slowly now,
Sliding through thought,
Tracing the outline of fear.
It isn't the clock that betrays you,
But the heart that counts alongside it.
In the stretch between ticks,
I lived lifetimes.
And in the tock that followed,
I forgot them all.
Drawn closer to some unknowable truth,
The rhythm is not yours to master.

Tock.

Kiss Me

Don't say goodbye.
It tastes like rusted keys in a lock I never asked to turn.
It smells like a book closing itself before the last line.
          Don't say goodbye, because if it's true, I won't manage.
          No. Say nothing. Let the silence be our map.
          I will follow the compass of your breath.
You, a comet with no orbit.
Me, the sky too small to hold you.
But still, we collide.
Not softly, but like a storm breaking through the bones of the sea.

Call it chaos. Call it fate. Call it nothing at all.

Kiss me like the clock has melted,
Like the hours have spilled onto the floor in a puddle of gold.
Kiss me like the world is unmade and we are its architects,
Drawing blueprints in the ashes of a sky too bright to survive.

Let the air forget how to carry sound.
Let the stars dim themselves in envy.
Let gravity stutter, unsure of its purpose.

But let your hands…
Oh, let your hands rewrite the story of what it means to stay.
Kiss me like the word never existed.

Turn "goodbye" into dust and scatter it in the wind.

Speak in fragments, in shapes, in colours.
Paint me a language no one else can understand,
Where every word begins with us and ends with always.

Kiss me.

Break the rules of what lips can do,
Teach them how to sing without sound.

Kiss me because we are unfinished.

Angels

I called for angels to come in the night,
To save me from shadows, to make it all right.
I stood on the edge, surrender in sight,
Begging for wings to soften my flight.

> Day after day, I whispered my plea,
> Prayers carved in silence, unanswered by thee.
> The void stretched wider, consuming my plea,
> And I learned that no one was coming for me.

Were they disgusted by the weight of my shame?
Did they see my wounds and shrink from the blame?
Or was their absence part of some cruel game,
To leave me alone in my smouldering flame?

> I waited for halos, for whispers of grace,
> For a hand to reach down and pull me from space.
> But the angels stayed hidden, refused to embrace,
> And I drowned in the depths of my own quiet place.

So now I walk through the dark on my own,
Through ashes and glass, with a heart made of stone.
No wings to lift me, no light to be shown,
Just me and the battle, the fight I've outgrown.

> Thank you, angels, for staying away,
> For proving no saviour would come here to stay.
> You taught me the truth in the harshest display:
> My strength is my own; I'll find my own way.

Mercy in Silence

We heard your cries, the whispers in the night,
Felt your pain, your struggle, your fading fight.
We saw you stand on that perilous height,
Begging for wings to make it all right.

> But love, it's not ours to pull you away,
> To force your hand or demand you stay.
> We offer no chains, no words to delay,
> For mercy is silent, it gives you your say.

You think we abandoned, turned cold to your plea,
But granting you freedom is true empathy.
To take your pain would mean you weren't free,
And love without choice is no love, you see.

> We watched as you teetered, the blade in your hand,
> Hoping you'd choose what we couldn't command.
> Your breath was your own, your choice to withstand,
> Not ours to decide, not ours to demand.

You stepped from the edge, not because of our grace,
But the strength you found in your quiet place.
The battle is yours, your own time to face,
A fire within, in this shadowed space.

> So, curse us if you must, for staying away,
> For letting the silence have its say.
> We loved you enough to let you decay,
> Hoping you'd find your own reason to stay.

Clouds

Not in the water but beneath it,
Breathing the upside-down skin of the sky.
River's pulse, like veins in the earth's wrist,
Their current humming secrets too ancient to list.

Lakes are not mirrors; they are windows,
Looking into a past where the rain remembers its name.
Raindrops fall not down, but inward,
Piercing the air's fabric like needles of liquid thread.

And the clouds,
The clouds are not clouds at all.
They are storytellers, amnesiac poets,
Carrying the weight of unwritten storms in their spines.
They unravel across the sky like whispered conspiracies,
Their shapes shifting with the indecision of dreams.
Each cloud is a hymn sung backward,
A canvas where the wind paints without hands.
They hover between the seen and unseen,
The first breath of chaos before the world awakens.

You?

You are not a cloud but the ghost of one,
You carry not rain but oceans folded into your pockets,
Their tides rising and falling to the rhythm of your pulse.

Without you, I am a sky emptied of wonder,
                                        A horizon that collapses inward.
I am dust orbiting nothing,
                        A shadow of something that was never there.

You are not just the origin,
                    You are the ending, the forgetting, the undone.

And I am left here,
looking up.
        Watching you scatter into

                                shapes   I can no
longer
        name.

Heart, Soul, and Mind

We are not bodies but fragments of storms,
Pieces of something that shattered before it was born.
A heart, a soul, a mind.
Not separate, but echoes of the same scream.

The heart is not
flesh; it is a king
without a crown,
A tyrant that rules
with no sense of
direction.
It beats not for
blood but for the
memory of rivers,
For the pulse of
things it will never
touch.

The soul is not light; it
is a shadow
pretending to glow,
A thief that steals
from the silence,
Carving its name into
the walls of the void,
Leaving trails that
lead nowhere but
back to itself.

The mind is not
thought; it is a
machine of mirrors,
Reflecting reflections
until truth dissolves.
It is the architect of
labyrinths,
Building questions it
dares not answer.

The heart wears the crown,
    The soul builds the throne,
        The mind draws the map.

                    But no one
                    follows.

We are confusion dressed as clarity,
                    A spark pretending to be fire.

We are a storm that spins, not to move,
                              But to keep itself alive.

          And when we f
                    a
                    l
                    l

When the pieces scatter into dust,
The heart will be the king who abandoned its kingdom.
The soul will be the thief who forgot what it stole.
The mind will be the mirror that shattered itself,
Trying to understand what it reflected.

Remember Me

Remember me when the moon hangs heavy and full,
When the rain slices the air like threads pulled taut.
Let the wind press its defiance against you,
                        And in its resistance, find my voice lingering.
When thunder shatters the sky in a raw, guttural cry,
And the clouds clash in battles unseen,
                        Think of me… not as absence,
                        But as the storm itself, restless and alive.

In the chaos above, feel my hand,
            not guiding, but steadying.
Though I may not be there to hold yours,
            I remain in the quiet you've forgotten how to hear.

Remember me when the earth beneath you trembles,
Not with fear, but with something profound.
When the world speaks in its oldest language,
Let it remind you of what we once shared.

And
If I am gone,
            When the storm recedes,
                        Look not for what was taken,
                                    But for what still stands.

Ruin

And so I stand in this fractured place,
Caught between ruins and the unknown

It is not hope that holds me still,
                                But the quiet rage

The will to survive, born of primal need,
Or the will to surrender, a planted seed.
Neither wrong, neither right.

A dead end carved by something unforgiving.
While time whispers of uncertain fates.
Ashes curl in the wind,
The echoes of what could have been.

So,
 I stand in this fractured place
         It is not hope that holds me still,
               Caught between ruins and the unknown
                     with nothing,
                                but the quiet rage

The Stranger
One day, I asked a man whose words were shaped like staircases:
"Where are you from?"
His face folded inward, collapsing into a smile too wide for his teeth,
And he answered in pieces, each one heavier than the last.
"I come from a place where the clocks run backward,
But only until you learn to stop watching.
Where silence isn't empty,
But overflows with the weight of forgotten sentences.
A place where doors do not lead anywhere,
But open anyway, just to ask if you're sure.
Where people speak in languages,
Built from the cracks in their own voices,
And no one minds if the words don't fit.
I come from a place where birds sing not to wake,
But to remind us that the sun is watching.
Where we do not sweeten what nature has given,
But take it as it is, raw and divine.
A place where the seasons do not argue with time,
Where mistakes are not flaws but murals,
Painted by the hands of those who dared to try,
A symphony of errors that hum in harmony."
His laughter was a jagged thing,
A sound that fell apart as soon as it was made.

I could feel it breaking between us,
Like glass pretending to be ice.
"Where is this place?" I asked,
Not because I wanted to go,
But because I already knew I couldn't.
"It isn't somewhere you find," he said,
"It's what's left when you stop trying.
You'll have to lose the name you never liked,
And all the names other people gave you, too.
Then there's the Bridge of Nothing.
You won't cross it; you'll build it as you go.
Every step is a piece of yourself you'll forget,
But only for as long as it takes to move forward.
There's a room you'll find,
Not by looking, but by letting it notice you.
Inside, there's a desk with no chair,
And a single sheet of paper that's already written itself.
When you read it, you'll understand:
It isn't the destination that matters,
It's the way the floor feels,
When you stop trying to stand still."
His answer wasn't over, but he had already stopped speaking.
And I realized then… He wasn't from a place at all.

He was the weight of a question,
I wasn't ready to carry.

9AM

It was 9AM, or so the clock claimed.
The bench beneath me felt older than the day,
Its wood worn smooth by the weight of others,
Who'd come here to find something they'd misplaced.

The rain wasn't just rain. It was deliberate,
A soft rhythm tapping out questions,
I didn't yet have answers for.

I sat, coffee
cooling in my
hand,
The steam
curling like
fleeting
thoughts
That refused
to take shape.

This bench,
This sturdy, unremarkable bench,
Held the kind of silence,
That wasn't empty.

Full of the lives it had cradled.
Full of the stillness I never allowed myself to feel.

I wasn't waiting for anyone. Not really.
                              The person I was waiting for was already here,
Sitting awkwardly, shifting restlessly in my chest.

The world was there but faint,
Damp leaves sticking to the ground,
Cars passing in muffled hums. A quiet pulse.

It was just me and this bench,
The only honest thing I'd sat on in years.
The bench didn't move, but it held me steady,
And for once, that was enough.

The rain pressed its rhythm into my skin,
The wood pressed its patience into my spine,
And I pressed my questions into the moment,
Letting it answer in its own slow way.

9 AM. Was it really then?
Or was it every hour that ever existed?

By the time I left,
I hadn't solved a single problem.
But I'd learned how to sit with them.

Light Is Coming Through
Once again, the light cuts through the curtains,
A quiet intruder slipping into my stillness.
I don't greet it. I'm not ready.
It waits anyway, patient and steady,
Like it knows I'll have to rise eventually.

Did I sleep?
It doesn't matter.
The hours blur, one
folding into another,
As if time itself
forgot what it was
doing.

I stand,
Not because I want to,
But because the day insists.

The sink greets me with cold water and colder reflection,
A face I know but don't quite recognize.
Shoes on, door open,
And I'm on the road.
                    Again.
            Not a road of adventure or destination,
            But the lonely stretch where I meet myself.

The city still sleeps,
Its breath rising in slow, smoky sighs.
The air tastes like yesterday,
And I'm a silhouette moving through its weight.
The walk is the same as always,
But today I carry something heavier.
A conversation I've avoided,
With myself,
About things I thought I'd forgotten.

Dear self,
Write it down, seal it,
And send it back to me in time.
Maybe one day I'll understand what you meant.
The light will come again tomorrow,
And the day after that.
It will keep insisting,
Keep slipping through the curtains,
Until I'm ready to greet it.

For now, I'll walk.
For now, I'll listen to the rhythm of the road,
And hope that someday,
The light finds its way through the thickest curtains of me.

Human Stripped

What are we beneath the layers we wear?
Not flesh, not bone, not the faces we prepare.
A heart? A mind? A soul in despair?
Or only the echoes of questions hanging in air?
Strip us deeper.
Past the skin, past the pulse,
Past the cages of ribs that clutch the muscle.
What's left?
A flicker, a thought, a word unsaid;
The residue of what we could have been.
The heart? It beats, but for what?
For love, for pain, for the things it forgot?
It wears a crown of fragile gold,
A king that's both too young and too old.
The mind? It calculates, it spins, it schemes.
But its brilliance is tangled in useless dreams.
It holds no answers, only doors;
Each leading back to the room before.
The soul? A vapor, a thread, a trace,
More absence than presence, more void than place.
It drifts, untethered, undefined,
The light that bends but cannot shine.
Strip us further,
What remains?

Not love, not anger, not joy, not pain.
Just a will.
To breathe, to endure, to claw through the noise,
To make meaning of things that refuse to explain themselves.
Perhaps that's all we are:
Not beings, but choices.
Not bodies, but the collisions of moments,
A mosaic made of splintered voices.
Human stripped;
We are not less, but more.
For when everything is taken,
Only the truth remains,
Even if it's hollow.

Bang, Can You Hear This?

Bang.

A sound that isn't just a sound,
But a punctuation mark punched
into
silence.

It
ricochets
off
the   walls of
my
mind

shaking l o o   s   e

thoughts,

I thought
were

an
ch

ored.

It's familiar now,
Dreams breaking apart mid-flight.
It's the sound of crystal shattering, not from weakness,
But because it was too sharp to hold itself together.

Even the pen in my hand trembles with the echo,
The ink bleeding faster as if to escape.
The letters I write stumble over themselves,
A staccato script that screams louder than words.
        My posture shifts; *the world tilts.*

I don't stir sugar into my coffee anymore. The cup feels heavy, foreign.
Like it belongs to someone else's hands.
I used to build dreams from glass,
Clear, strong, untouchable.
But glass, when it breaks,
Doesn't just shatter. It cuts.
Deep.

                        Bang.

Can you hear it?
Perhaps you can see different?
It's simple:
        The sun doesn't set, the ocean drowns it.

Removal of Time
I've cast the clock from this hollow space,
No ticking heart to fill its place.
No hands to carve the hours apart,
No seconds to tear at a fragile heart.
The silence grows, not calm, but loud,
A shapeless weight, a heavy shroud.
Fog creeps in with a question untold,
Is this freedom, or chains grown cold?
Through the curtains, a blood-red glow,
Morning or dusk? I'll never know.
The light doesn't brighten; it burns instead,
Painting the room in a fiery thread.
My body stays, locked to the chair,
My mind wanders, but it finds nowhere.
My heart beats on, but skips its tune,
A rebel drum in a lifeless room.
No time to break, no time to mend,
No start to begin, no end to end.
Just me, the pen, and a world confined,
A hollow echo of an absent mind.
Outside, the world may rise or fall,
I wouldn't know, I've abandoned it all.
No ticking hands, no measured climb,
Just the strange, raw stillness of removing time.

This Crazy Heart
What am I supposed to do with this heart?
It isn't mine; it never was.
It's a storm trapped in glass,
A sharp, untamed thing pretending to be fragile.

> This heart waits in the silence between seconds,
> Even when the world has already moved on.
> It carries its secrets like stones in its chest,
> Heavy but precious, a burden it refuses to drop.

It loves like fire loves the wood,
Like waves love the shore,
With no care for the damage it leaves behind.

This heart doesn't hesitate to tear itself apart,
For a glance, a touch,
For the impossible weight of someone else's name.
It bleeds without flinching,
And calls it devotion.

> Broken isn't the right word.
> It doesn't shatter; it twists, bends,
> Turns its scars into directions,
> For places it never should have gone.

And yet, it keeps beating.
Not for itself, but for the possibility:

For the hope of
          being seen,
          being held.

Even if it means breaking
          all over again.

Again

Me again,
     You again.
               Not a beginning, not an end,
                    A loop that doesn't ask for escape.
This time isn't about love,
It's about the silence love leaves behind.
It's about the questions we don't dare ask,
And the answers we can't hold without breaking.

     It slips through us,
     Like water pretending to be solid?
     I don't know.
     But I want to try.

There's something in the way you stand,
The way you look past me but never through.
It's in the way your hand hovers near mine,
As if the distance is the only thing keeping us real.

          So here we are again.
          A beginning disguised as an ending,
          A moment that feels like forever,
          And tomorrow all at once.

Take my hand.
　　　　Let's find out
what we can
　　　　create.

Too Late

Laugh while you can, while the days are still kind,
Before the weight of the world tangles your mind.
Play in the sunlight, let joy be your song,
For tomorrow will come, and it won't take long.

    You've never met sadness, not face to face,
    Nor felt the chill of an empty space.
    You've never known nights that refuse to end,
    Or the silence that settles when you lose a friend.

Laugh while you can, before time takes its toll,
Before it carves lines that echo your soul.
The speed of tomorrow will steal what you know,
And leave you with shadows wherever you go.

    You'll see and you'll hear what you never could bear,
    Feel the weight of the past in the cold, heavy air.
    You'll long for the days when you couldn't speak,
    When innocence lived in the soft and the meek.

Too late to return, too late to erase,
Too late to relive that untainted space.
The laughter has faded, replaced by the years,
And the mirror reflects both your joy and your tears.

Random Day
The wind didn't howl, it whispered,
Running its invisible fingers along the edges of the world.
The sun wasn't blazing; it hovered,
An indifferent watcher, spilling light without care.
The sky, bare and blue, seemed absent-minded,
As if it had forgotten what clouds were meant to do.
The day moved forward, not with purpose,
But with the quiet inevitability of a clock
That neither rushes nor waits.
The bench beneath me wasn't special,
But in its stillness, it became profound.
The ticking of the world didn't distract;
It softened, folded itself into the corners of the moment.
There was no story here.

No grand revelation, no seismic shift.
Just time, unfolding itself in tiny pieces,
And me, realizing that I was allowed to hold them.
I sat there, not thinking,
Just feeling the air press lightly against my skin,
The warmth of the sun curling into the coolness of shade.
It wasn't perfect.
It wasn't trying to be.

And maybe,
that was the lesson.
That life,
is less about chasing
what matters.

And more about,
Noticing the things,
that don't ask,
to be noticed at all.